GROWING INFORMAL CITIES PROJECT

MIGRANT ENTREPRENEURSHIP COLLECTIVE VIOLENCE AND XENOPHOBIA IN SOUTH AFRICA

JONATHAN CRUSH AND SUJATA RAMACHANDRAN

MIGRATION POLICY SERIES NO. 67

SERIES EDITOR:
PROF. JONATHAN CRUSH

SOUTHERN AFRICAN MIGRATION PROGRAMME (SAMP)
INTERNATIONAL MIGRATION RESEARCH CENTRE (IMRC)
2014

Acknowledgements

We wish to thank the International Development Research Centre (IDRC) for funding the Growing Informal Cities Project, a partnership between SAMP, the African Centre for Cities (UCT), the International Migration Research Centre (Balsillie School of International Affairs), the Gauteng City Regional Observatory and Eduardo Mondlane University (Mozambique). Our thanks for their assistance with this report to Bronwen Dachs, Maria Salamone, Abel Chikanda and Caroline Skinner.

Contents Page

List of Tables Page

LIST OF FIGURES   PAGE

EXECUTIVE SUMMARY

The remarkable growth of informal migrant entrepreneurship in South Africa since 1990 would have been much lauded had it not been for the striking detail that the actors in question are seen as "foreigners" or "outsiders". As such, they are uniformly viewed as undesirable and disadvantaging poor South African citizens. The growing presence of migrants in the informal sector has created various tensions in South Africa, including in government circles, ignoring the fact that in the free market economy of South Africa, immigrants and refugees, like citizens and commercial enterprises, would otherwise enjoy the freedom to establish, operate and expand their businesses.

The xenophobic anti-immigrant violence that swept South Africa in May 2008 led to the deaths of over 70 people, seriously injured 400 and displaced as many as 100,000 from their communities. A large number of migrant-owned businesses were also destroyed in the mayhem. Looting, burning and destruction of business property was widespread and many migrant entrepreneurs were among those hounded out of their communities.

Such actions did not stop after May 2008, however. If anything, they have become more insidious and pervasive.

South Africa provides an important case study of how citizen attitudes and behaviours materially affect the business climate for migrant entrepreneurs. Trying to run a business in the informal economy is an especially hazardous undertaking in South Africa. First, the state (both central and municipal) has adopted a protectionist position, which leads to various regulatory and policing responses that seek to disadvantage, if not eliminate, migrant entrepreneurship. Second, the police run their own protection (or non-harassment) rackets to benefit financially from those able to pay. Third, South African competitors, particularly in the spaza sector, have increasingly adopted a strategy of using violence to intimidate and drive migrant entrepreneurs out of an area. And fourth, a minority of citizens have turned hostile attitudes towards migrants and refugees into violent actions by forcibly shutting down migrant-owned businesses and attacking their owners and employees. Underlying all of these responses is a strong xenophobic undertow.

National attitudinal surveys by SAMP, as well as in-depth qualitative research and the personal testimony of many migrants, confirm that many South Africans hold deep-rooted negative opinions about migrants and migrant entrepreneurs. In the face of this body of evidence, claims by prominent political figures that xenophobia does not exist in South Africa ring extremely hollow. South Africans make clear distinctions between African migrants of different nationalities, with migrants from countries including Somalia and Zimbabwe viewed far less favourably than those from Botswana, Lesotho and Swaziland. Since many informal migrant entrepreneurs are from Zimbabwe, Mozambique, Somalia and the DRC, they are singled out for harsh treatment.

SAMP asked South Africans how likely they would be to take part in collective action against the presence of migrants and found 25% were likely to prevent a migrant from operating a business in their area. The survey results revealed that around one in every ten South Africans was predisposed to turn hostile attitudes into violent actions. This may seem a relatively low proportion in light of the prevalence of negative attitudes but multiplied it suggests that 3.8 million (out of an adult population of around 35 million) South Africans would be prepared to use violent means to rid their neighbourhoods of foreign migrants.

Looting and vandalism of migrant-owned shops have been especially common features of collective violence over the past several years. Some of this violence is obviously motivated primarily by criminality, especially robberies and looting, but to attribute all attacks to criminal motivation is reductionist and misleading. In general, the weak structural and social position of "foreigners" in localized areas as "outsiders", combined with limited access to protection and justice, makes them more vulnerable to criminal attack. Acts of collective violence include (a) written or verbal threats and insults directed at migrant entrepreneurs; (b) public intimidation of migrant entrepreneurs through protests or marches or other similar collective actions; (c) involuntary migrant shop closures; (d) direct physical violence against migrant store owners or their employees; (e) looting of store contents; (f) damage to the physical structure of shops, especially through arson; (g) damage or destruction of other property belonging to migrant traders, including homes and cars; (h) temporary or permanent forced displacement of migrant entrepreneurs and their families; and (i) extortion for protection by local leaders, police and residents. Looting of store goods and damage to the stores were easily the most common types of action recorded.

While xenophobic views and actions are not espoused or approved of by all local residents of affected settlements, their prevalence suggests that they do enjoy sufficient support and that there are few deterrents. Far from reducing xenophobia, claims that collective violence against migrant businesses are simply acts of criminality legitimize and may even incite further violence. There is also the prejudiced, xenophobic idea that non-citizens are not entitled to anything – not police protection and certainly not to run a small business, even if it is enshrined in law and generated through their own initiative. The bigger picture, which includes the threat to all small-scale traders posed by supermarkets' increasing dominance, is lost as the focus turns to curtailing migrant entrepreneurship in place of the real, urgent need to support opportunities for *all* small entrepreneurs in marginal settlements through incentives and programmes.

This report focuses on the chronology and geography of collective violence against migrant entrepreneurs since South Africa's first democratic elections in 1994. The overall aim of the research was to document and create a chronological account of attacks on migrant businesses, to categorise the types and frequency of attacks and to map the locations where such events occurred. The incidents discussed involve the intentional and spontaneous participation of groups of people in acts of collective violence against migrant businesses. Three distinct criteria, singly or in combination, were used for including an incident as part of the analysis: first, the scale of damage had to be extensive, affecting a number of businesses; second, there had to have been displacement of and injuries to business owners; and third, the violence had to have been perpetrated by groups rather than individuals. The analysis revealed the following about attacks on migrant entrepreneurs:

- There has been a marked pattern of escalation over time. Pre-2005 incidents constitute less than 5% of recorded episodes. A definite upswing is seen from 2006 onwards, with the sharpest growth occurring after 2008. Excluding events in May 2008, nearly 90% of recorded episodes of group violence against migrant businesses occurred since the beginning of 2008. The five years with the largest number of incidents were from 2010 to 2014.

- Collective violence targeting migrant entrepreneurs is no longer confined to a few isolated locations. Since 2005, the majority of South African provinces have been touched by such collective violence. However, the Western Cape and Gauteng have experienced the highest levels of violence. The overall number of affected provinces and localities has increased considerably since 2005 and the majority of provinces have witnessed repeated incidents since 2009. Since 2009, at least 32 distinct locations have witnessed two or more episodes of group violence.

- The scale of the attacks is sometimes sizeable and can spill over into neighbouring settlements. Looting and vandalism of migrant-owned shops have been especially common features of collective violence. These actions, though criminal, may appear less grave when compared to severe injuries and loss of lives, but they cannot be treated as inconsequential as they impose unwarranted hardships on migrant entrepreneurs through partial or complete loss of stock and destruction of their shops and investments.

- Collective violence against migrant businesses also impacts negatively on South African citizens and businesses. Wholesalers, retailers and suppliers are affected when migrant business activities are disrupted or destroyed. Also, a significant proportion of migrant businesses rent business spaces from South African property owners, who lose rental income when their tenants are expelled or their premises are vandalized. Other losers include poor local consumers who are forced to buy more expensive goods from larger stores or face the inconvenience of travelling longer distances to purchase necessities.

3

The opinions of politicians and officials about migrant entrepreneurs often seem indistinguishable from the intolerant views of ordinary citizens and this, in turn, reinforces negative beliefs and ideas in the populace at large. Their excusing attacks on migrant entrepreneurs as unrelated to xenophobia are contradicted by the details of many of these attacks. What makes the official position especially ironic is when officials themselves articulate sentiments that reproduce the xenophobic myths that they claim do not exist. Failure to curb the situation by consistently restraining offenders and imposing stringent penalties on collective violence only expands the elements of "opportunism" attached to such acts, encouraging others to participate, and reinforcing the unprotected position of migrants and refugees as "outsiders" in affected areas.

"Are we so despised that because I sell a loaf of bread a little cheaper than my competitor I must be punished for it with my life?".[1]

INTRODUCTION

International migrants are often lauded for their enterprise, innovation and business acumen.[2] However, it is clear that these "unsung heroes" face formidable obstacles in successfully establishing and growing an enterprise in a new country of settlement.[3] Common economic and social challenges confronting small-scale immigrant entrepreneurs from the Global South include limited market information, low levels of personal liquidity, poor access to credit and startup capital, high transaction costs, gender discrimination, over-regulation and intense competition.[4] The national and local policy environment within which immigrant businesses operate also plays a critical role in determining business failure or success. The environment includes legal restrictions and obligations, attitudes and policies towards migrant business activity, immigration and refugee legislation, and policing practices. As one study of immigrant entrepreneurial behaviour notes, "the effects of the regulatory environment are transmitted through a broad range of state activities, including through the knock-on effect of immigration laws, which may not have had an intended influence".[5]

While some attention has been given to the economic and policy environment in explaining variations in business performance among immigrant entrepreneurs, much less has been paid to how the negative reactions of citizens to their activities and presence in the country might impact on entrepreneurship.[6] South Africa provides a particularly important case study of how citizen attitudes and behaviours materially affect the business climate for migrant entrepreneurs. In August 1997, for example, in the midst of "rainbow nation" euphoria following the country's first democratic elections, non-South African street traders were attacked and assaulted on the streets of Johannesburg. Many lost their merchandise and stands, some at gunpoint. The violence and intimidation were "accompanied by angry and vitriolic anti-immigrant rhetoric".[7] This incident, largely overlooked by the state, emboldened a pattern of hostility towards migrant entrepreneurs that has reached epidemic proportions over the last decade.

Sometimes lost in the sobering statistics about the anti-immigrant violence that swept South Africa in May 2008 (over 70 people dead, 400 seriously injured, and 100,000 internally displaced) is the fact that many migrant-owned businesses were caught up in the mayhem.[8] Looting, burning and destruction of business property was widespread in the affected areas and many migrant entrepreneurs were among those hounded out of their communities. Such actions did not die out after May 2008. If anything, as this report demonstrates, they have become more insidious and pervasive, and are certainly not confined to the areas that erupted in 2008.

The remarkable growth of informal migrant entrepreneurship in South Africa since 1990, its innovative strategies, and the kinship, ethnic and business networks through which goods are acquired and resources accumulated, would have been much lauded had it not been for the striking detail that the actors in question are "foreigners" or "outsiders". As such, they are seen as undesirable and disadvantaging poor South African citizens with meagre avenues for income generation and survival. The growing presence of migrants in the informal sector has created noticeable tension in various quarters in South Africa, including government circles, ignoring the fact that in the free market economy of South Africa, immigrants and refugees, like citizens and commercial enterprises, enjoy the freedom to establish, operate and expand their businesses.[9]

Successive national attitudinal surveys by SAMP since 1996, as well as in-depth qualitative research and the personal testimony of many migrants, leave little doubt that South Africans hold deep-rooted negative opinions about migrants and refugees in general and migrant entrepreneurs in particular.[10] In the face of this body of evidence, recurrent denials by prominent political figures that xenophobia exists ring especially hollow.[11] Migrants and refugees interfacing with state institutions in various sectors report that these interactions are infused with attitudes and rhetoric that question their right to be in the country and regularly lead to the denial of services to which they are entitled by law and the constitution. Furthermore, when the majority of South Africans in national opinion surveys believe that refugees and migrants should not be entitled to legal and police protection, it is perhaps unsurprising that only the most egregious cases of police brutality garner public sympathy and attention – and even then only because they happen to be caught on video.

The first part of this report presents the results of SAMP's most recent survey of South African attitudes towards migrants and refugees on the linkages between negative attitudes and hostile behaviours. In other words, how willing are South Africans to actually do something about the perceived "threat" of migrants and what measures are they willing to take? This analysis provides the context for understanding the problems confronting migrant entrepreneurs. The second section describes and analyses the nature of what we call "extreme xenophobia"; that is, the prevalence of physical violence against migrant entrepreneurs in South Africa.[12] This report focuses on the frequency and incidence of collective xenophobic violence, its impact on migrant entrepreneurship and the evasions of the authorities.

A DANGEROUS CLIMATE

Being perceived as a 'foreigner' in post-apartheid South Africa (particularly if one is from another African country) is inherently dangerous, so pervasive is the feeling amongst ordinary South Africans that you do not belong and should "go home".[13] Trying to run a business in the South African informal economy is an especially hazardous undertaking as there is a widespread perception that migrant entrepreneurial activities inevitably disadvantage South Africans. This perception has been acted on in four main ways. First, the state (both central and municipal) has adopted a "protectionist" position, which leads to various regulatory and policing responses that seek to disadvantage, if not entirely eliminate, migrant entrepreneurship.[14] Second, the police on the streets run their own protection (or non-harassment) rackets to benefit financially from those able to pay. Third, South African competitors, particularly in the spaza sector, have increasingly adopted a strategy of what Charman and Piper call "violent entrepreneurship"; that is, the use of violence to intimidate and drive migrants entrepreneurs out of an area.[15] Fourth, a minority of citizens have turned hostile attitudes into violent actions by forcibly shutting down migrant-owned businesses and attacking their owners and employees. Underlying all of these responses is a strong xenophobic undertow which is both manifest and measurable.

The World Values Survey (an independent global attitudinal survey) has consistently shown that South Africans are the least disposed globally to migrants coming from other countries to engage in economic activity. The most recent survey found that 30% of South Africans want a total prohibition on foreign migrants who intend to work in South Africa (easily the highest figure of any country surveyed) (Table 1). Nearly half (48%) want there to be strict limits on entry. Thus, 78% are basically opposed to the idea of economic immigration to the country; no other country in the South has more than 50%. South Africa (at 16%) also has the lowest proportion of people in favour of skills-based immigration to fill gaps in the local job market and the lowest number (6%) who favour an open-door policy towards economic migration.

SAMP's periodic surveys of South African attitudes towards the impacts of migration reveal more of the underlying economic hostility towards migrants (Table 2). Although there have been changes over time (with negative perceptions peaking in 2006), there has been a general growth in negativity about the social and economic impacts of migration since the 1990s. Between 1999 and 2010, for example, the proportion of South Africans who agreed that migrants use up resources increased from 59% to 63%. Those agreeing that they were responsible for crime increased from 45% to 55% and those that they bring disease from 24% to 39%. In terms of economic impacts, those agreeing that they deprive South Africans of jobs has remained steady at around 60%. The proportion who felt that migrants bring skills needed by South Africa plummeted from 58% in 1999 to 34% in 2010. Only a quarter agree that migrants actually create jobs for South Africans.

Table 1: South African Attitudes To Economic Migrants in Comparative Perspective				
Country	Prohibit immigration (%)	Place strict limits on entry (%)	Let people in as long as jobs are available (%)	Let in anyone who wants to enter (%)
South				
South Africa	30	48	16	6
India	23	23	25	30
Ghana	18	39	36	7
Zambia	11	30	44	15
Brazil	11	33	47	9
China	8	21	51	20
Indonesia	6	15	72	8
Thailand	5	16	65	14
Malaysia	2	8	72	18
North				
Italy	8	49	37	6
United States	7	37	49	8
Germany	7	43	45	5
Australia	3	54	41	2
Canada	2	39	51	8
Source: World Values Survey				

Table 2: South African Perceptions of Impacts of Migration*			
	1999 (%)	2006 (%)	2010 (%)
Social impacts			
Use up resources (e.g. water, electricity, housing)	59	67	63
Commit crime	45	67	55
Bring disease	24	49	39
Economic impacts			
Take jobs	56	62	60
Bring needed skills	58	25	34
Create jobs for South Africans	–	22	27
*Percentage who agree/strongly agree			

Because migrants in South Africa come from all over the world it is important to know if particular opprobrium is reserved for those from certain areas. In the latest SAMP survey, migrants from other Southern African countries had the highest favourability ratings (25% "completely favourable"), followed by migrants from Europe and North America (21%) and the rest of Africa (17%) (Table 3). Differences therefore exist but they are not particularly large and all migrants, wherever they are from, rate much lower than South Africans' evaluations of themselves (65% favourable for Black South Africans and 56% favourable for White South Africans). Since a significant number of migrants (and migrant entrepreneurs) are refugees, it is of interest that only 21% of South Africans have a completely favourable impression of refugees. Unsurprisingly, irregular migrants are viewed with the most distaste (12% favourable and 49% completely unfavourable).

Table 3: South African Impressions of Migrants and Citizens, 2010		
	Completely favourable (%)	Completely unfavourable (%)
South African groups		
Blacks	65	5
Whites	56	4
Coloureds	49	7
Indians/Asians	42	12
Migrant groups		
Southern Africans	25	21
Europeans/North Americans	21	18
Rest of Africa	17	26
Refugees/asylum-seekers	21	27
Irregular migrants	12	49

South Africans do make clear distinctions between African migrants of different nationalities (Table 4). Within the SADC region, migrants from Botswana, Lesotho and Swaziland are viewed more positively than those from Zimbabwe and Mozambique. However, migrants from non-neighbouring countries rate even less positively: Nigerians (59% unfavourable), Congolese (51% unfavourable) and Somalis (50% unfavourable). Since many informal migrant entrepreneurs are drawn from the ranks of Zimbabweans, Mozambicans, Somalis and Congolese, it is not hard to imagine why they are singled out for harsh treatment. SAMP also found that levels of xenophobia are highest amongst self-employed South Africans in the informal economy.[16] Levels are lower amongst both the unemployed and employees in the informal economy.

Table 4: South African Impressions of Migrants by Country of Origin, 2010		
	Unfavourable (%)	Favourable (%)
Neighbouring countries		
Zimbabwe	44	15
Mozambique	40	15
Botswana	24	31
Swaziland	23	33
Lesotho	23	32
Other African countries		
Nigeria	59	7
Angola	48	9
DRC	51	9
Somalia	50	9
Ghana	45	11

Simply because the majority of a national population hold negative perceptions of a minority group such as migrants, it does not automatically follow that violent acts against that group will be pervasive or, indeed, occur at all. However, a significant minority of South Africans polled in attitudinal surveys have consistently expressed a willingness to take the law into their own hands. In 2010, for example, SAMP asked South Africans how likely they would be to take part in collective action against migrants (Table 5). As many as 23% said it was likely that they would act to stop migrants moving into their community, 20% would prevent migrant children enrolling in the same schools as their own children, and 15% would prevent migrants from becoming co-workers. Important for the argument of this report, 25% said they would be likely to stop a migrant from operating a business in their area.

By dividing respondents into those that lived in 'hotspots' in the May 2008 violence and those in areas that were not, it is possible to ascertain if areas with experience of widespread violence are more prone to future violence.[17] While hotspot residents are more likely to prevent migrants from operating a business and moving into their community, they are less likely to oppose them becoming co-workers or enrolling their children in the same schools. However, the differences are not large and one in four residents of areas not directly affected by May 2008 said they were likely to take action to stop a migrant from operating a business in their community.

Table 5: Likelihood of South Africans Taking Preventative Action Against Migrants, 2010			
How likely are you to take action to prevent migrants doing the following: (% Likely/Very likely)	All urban areas	2008 hotspots	2008 other
From operating a business in your area	25	27	24
From moving into your neighbourhood	23	27	21
From enrolling their children in school	20	18	21
From becoming a co-worker	15	14	21

Finally, the SAMP survey asked South Africans how likely they would be to take certain actions against people they suspected were irregular migrants in their community. Since South Africans believe that the vast majority of foreign migrants are in the country illegally, this is not very different to asking what they would do about migrants in general. Around a third said they would report them to the police, to employers or to community leaders (Table 6). Fewer (15%) said they would combine with others to eject them from the community and 11% said they were prepared to use violence against the migrants. The predilection to use violence was actually slightly stronger in areas not affected by the attacks of May 2008. What this means is that around one in every ten South Africans is predisposed to turn hostile attitudes into violent actions. This may seem a relatively low proportion in light of the prevalence of negative attitudes but multiplied it does suggest that 3.8 million (out of an adult population of around 35 million) South Africans would be prepared to use violent means to rid their neighbourhoods of foreign migrants.

Table 6: Likelihood of Taking Punitive Action Against Irregular Migrants, 2010			
How likely are you to take action against irregular migrants in your area: (% Likely/Very likely)	All urban areas	2008 hotspots	2008 other
Report them to police	36	34	36
Report them to employer	27	26	28
Report them to community association	27	24	29
Combine to force them to leave	15	15	15
Use violence against them	11	9	11

METHODOLOGY

There has been no systematic longitudinal analysis of the nature, distribution and intensity of violent incidents targeting migrants and refugees. Official statistics are not maintained and the tendency of government representatives and senior politicians to classify violent attacks on migrants and migrant businesses as "opportunistic crime" has only deepened the uncertainty about the occurrence of xenophobic violence in the country and its underlying causes.[18] This report draws on the evidence from an extensive archive of news articles from various media sources collected by SAMP since 1994 and detailed timeline reconstructions already in the public domain.[19] The overall aim of the research was to create a chronological account of attacks on migrant businesses, to categorise the types and frequency of attacks and to map the locations where such events occurred.

Several qualifications are in order. First, research on hate crimes in other contexts confirms that a sizeable proportion of such episodes go unreported and unrecorded.[20] The inventory on which this paper is based does not claim to be exhaustive since many incidents undoubtedly go unreported by the press or human rights groups. Second, the lack of confidence in law enforcement agencies, poor prosecution of offenders, weak deterrent measures for xenophobic violence, as well as the continued presence of offenders in localized settings, are all likely to discourage migrants from reporting to the authorities.[21] Third, the information in the database tends to be descriptive in nature, describing but not explaining why attacks take place or why they take the particular form that they do.

Although there is plenty of evidence of violent attacks on individual migrant entrepreneurs, this paper focuses on acts of collective or group violence. Collective violence has been defined as the "instrumental use of violence by persons who define themselves as members of a group against another group in order to achieve political, social or economic objectives".[22] Aggressive social interaction organized on a group basis is the key feature here, whether this group or collective identity is assumed and transitory or has a permanent and stable character. This form of episodic social interaction involves perpetrators who distinguish themselves from the targeted victims either subliminally or directly. Moreover, this contact directly inflicts physical damage on the targeted persons and/or their possessions with some level of coordination and synchronization amongst the perpetrators, even in incidents that appear spontaneous with low levels of organization.[23] There are obviously different varieties of collective violence, varying in scope, duration and degree of organization. The damage caused by such violence also varies in scale and gravity with some acts having far-reaching and deadly consequences, such as those that swept South Africa in May 2008.[24]

Collective violence has also been defined as a type of social control in which grievances and perceived wrongs are handled through unilateral aggression.[25] The collectivization of violence generally occurs where there is strong partisanship and additional individuals support one side against the other. Solidarity is skewed in favour of the perpetrators and distanced from the targets of violence.[26] A high frequency of collective violence is an indicator of profound social and cultural distance between the groups involved (the perpetrators and their intended targets). Other localized factors such as low institutional confidence, weak policing, and areas with long histories of violent crime, buttress a social environment where the likelihood and opportunities for collective violence remain robust.[27] Institutional barriers to protection and justice for the victims activate and perpetuate the violence.

The incidents discussed in this paper involve the intentional and spontaneous participation of groups of people in acts of collective violence against migrant businesses. The SAMP database contains information on over 250 separate incidents of collective violence since 1994. Migrant entrepreneurs and their businesses were also severely affected during the large-scale violence that occurred in May 2008. However, the events of that month are excluded from this assessment since they have been examined in depth elsewhere and are often treated as an exceptionally large singular event, even though there were at least 100 (and perhaps as many as 150) localized incidents of collective violence.[28] The assessment is based on the identification and analysis of the largest or most significant episodes occurring since 1994. Three distinct criteria, singly or in combination, were used for inclusion: first, the scale of damage had to be extensive, affecting a number of businesses; second, there had to have been displacement of and injuries to business owners; and third, the violence had to have been perpetrated by groups rather than individuals.

COLLECTIVE VIOLENCE AGAINST MIGRANT ENTREPRENEURS

CHRONOLOGY OF COLLECTIVE VIOLENCE

From 1994 to August 2014 (excluding May 2008), there were at least 250 documented episodes of group-based violence against migrants and refugee businesses in various locations around the country. The actual tally is likely to be even higher since not all events reach the attention of the media and monitoring organizations. An analysis of the frequency of collective violence reveals a marked pattern of escalation over time (Table 7).

Table 7: Frequency of Collective Violence		
Year	No. of incidents	Percentage
Pre-2005	9	4
2005	4	2
2006	9	4
2007	9	4
2008*	19	8
2009	17	7
2010	46	20
2011	22	10
2012	25	11
2013	36	16
2014 (to end-August)	32	14
Total	228	100
* Excluding May 2008 attacks		

Pre-2005 incidents constitute less than 5% of recorded episodes. A definite upswing is seen from 2006 onwards, with the sharpest growth occurring after 2008. Excluding events in May 2008, nearly 90% of recorded episodes of group violence against migrant businesses occurred since the beginning of 2008. The five years with the largest number of incidents were from 2010 to 2014. The highest annual number (20% of the total) was recorded in 2010 during an upsurge in xenophobic attacks after the World Cup was held in South Africa. While these episodes differed in terms of the number of affected migrants and the severity of the damage, it is evident that small-scale, informal migrant businesses occupy a highly precarious position in South African settlements, having become especially vulnerable to situations of collective violence.

GEOGRAPHIES OF COLLECTIVE VIOLENCE

Collective violence targeting migrant entrepreneurs is no longer confined to a few isolated locations. Since 2005, the majority of South African provinces have been touched by collective violence against migrant businesses. However, the Western Cape and Gauteng have experienced the highest levels of violence. The overall number of affected provinces and localities has increased considerably since 2005; indeed, the majority of provinces have witnessed repeated incidents since 2009. In 2005-2006, incidents occurred in six distinct locations within three provinces (Figure 1). In 2009-2010, they occurred in at least 14 separate locations extending over six of the nine provinces in South Africa (Figures 2 to 4). The year 2010 stands out with at least 37 separate locations situated in six provinces. The number of affected areas may have fallen somewhat to 22 in 2012 and 27 in 2013, but the number of affected provinces still stood at 6 and 7 respectively (Figures 5 to 7).

Several of the affected locations have witnessed repeated rounds of collective violence. Diepsloot, for example, was affected in 2006, and again in 2009, 2010 and 2013.[29] Other areas have experienced several incidents with short intervals between them. In the town of Delmas in Mpumalanga, for example, migrant businesses were assailed in February 2013 and again in April that year. In Mamelodi, migrant businesses were attacked in June 2014 and again in September. Since 2009, at least 32 distinct locations have witnessed two or more episodes of group violence (Table 8). Of these, collective violence has been repeated on three or more occasions in 12 areas: Delmas, Diepsloot, Duduza, Gugulethu, Khayelitsha, KwaNobuhle, Langa, Mamelodi, Motherwell, Orange Farm, Ramaphosa and Soweto. Some of these locations, such as Ramaphosa township, also witnessed extensive violence and destruction during May 2008.[30]

Table 8: Collective Violence Locations, 2009–2014	
Locations	Province
Booysens Park, KwaDesi, KwaNobuhle, Kugya, Motherwell, Port Elizabeth	Eastern Cape
Bothaville, Botshabelo, Deneysville, Fouriesburg, Koppies, Kroonstad, Maokeng, Odendaalsrus, Sasolburg, Thabong, Viljoenskroon, Welkom, Zamdela	Free State
Atteridgeville, Benoni, Boipatong, Diepsloot, Duduza, Ekurhuleni, Evaton, Fochville, Freedom Park, Ga-Rankuwa, Imbeliseni, Johannesburg, Kya Sands, Lakeside, Mamelodi, Mayfair, Orange Farm, Protea, Ramaphosa, Ratanda, Sebokeng, Sharpeville, Soshanguve, Soweto, Tembisa, Thokoza, Tsakane	Gauteng
Giyani, Marapong, Phagemeng, Lebowakgomo, Lephalale	Limpopo
Botshabelo, Delmas, Emjindini, Leandra, Mhluzi, Sakhile, Siyathemba	Mpumalanga
Barkly West	Northern Cape
Boitekong, Boitumelong, Rustenburg, Setlagole	North West
Bishop Lavis, Bloekombos, Botrivier, Cape Town, Delft, Du Noon, Franschhoek, Freedom Park, Grabouw, Gugulethu, Harare, Khayelitsha, Klapmuts, Langa, Malmesbury, Mbekweni, Mitchells Plain, Moorreesburg, Nyanga, Paarl East, Philippi, Riviersonderend, Samora Machel, Silverton, Valhalla Park, Wellington, Wolseley, Worcester	Western Cape

Figure 1: Collective Violence Locations, South Africa 2005–2006

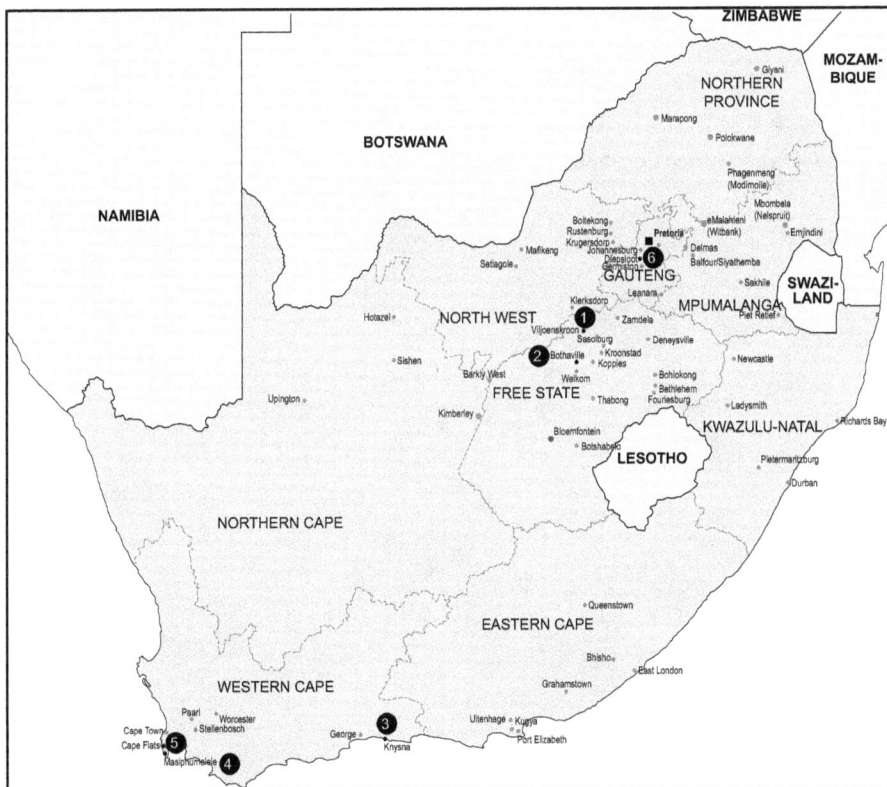

Figure 2: Collective Violence Locations, South Africa 2009–2010

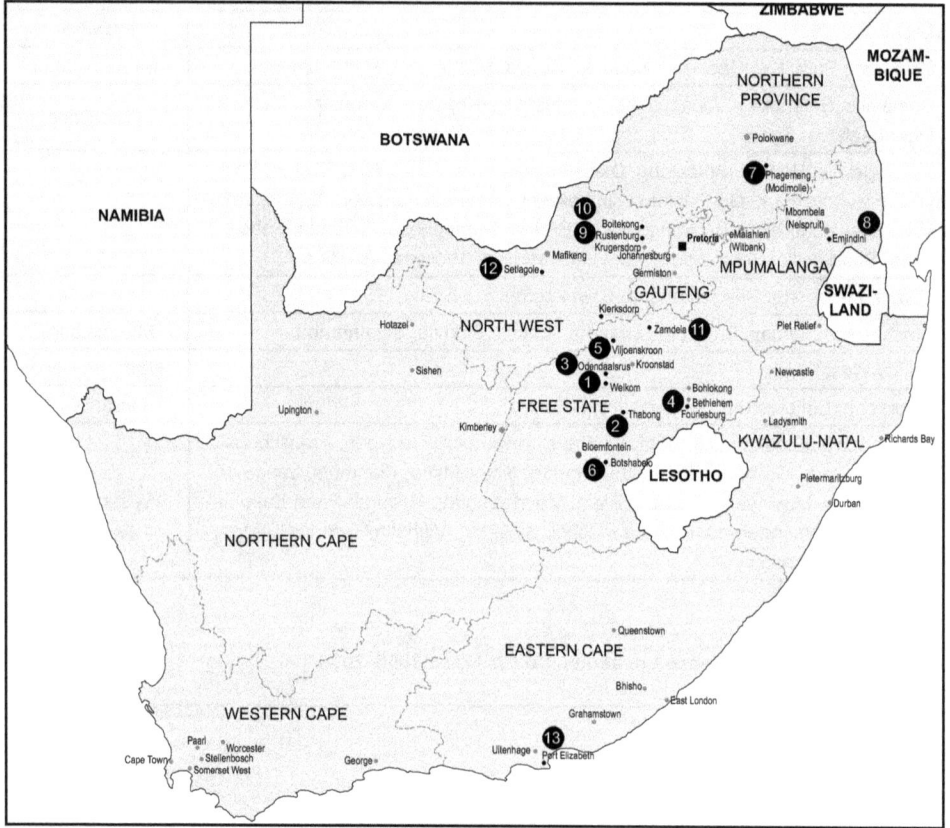

Figure 3: Collective Violence Locations, Gauteng 2009–2010

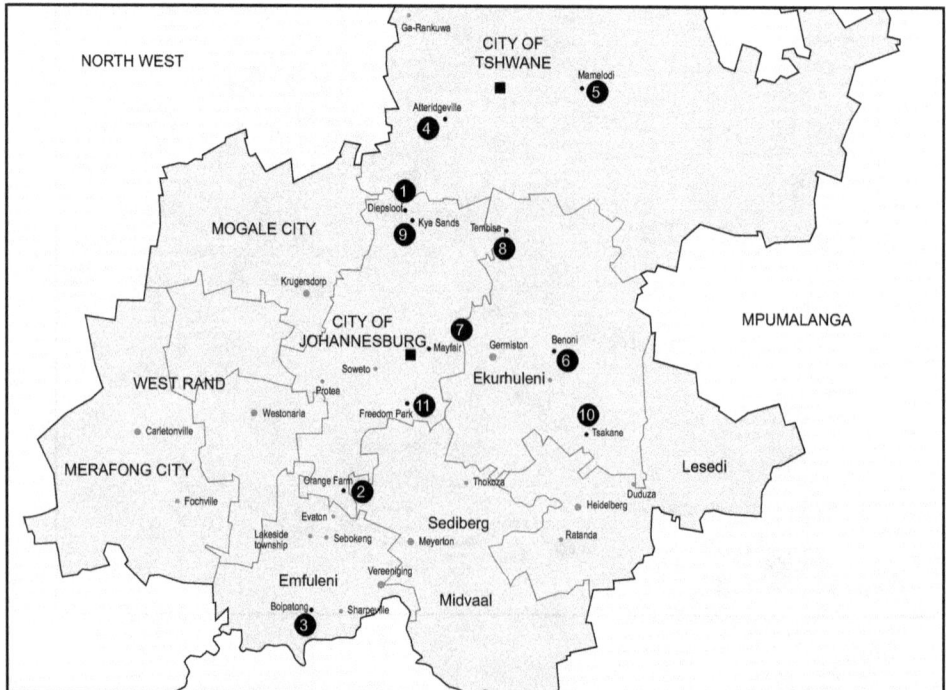

Figure 4: Collective Violence Locations, Western Cape 2009–2010

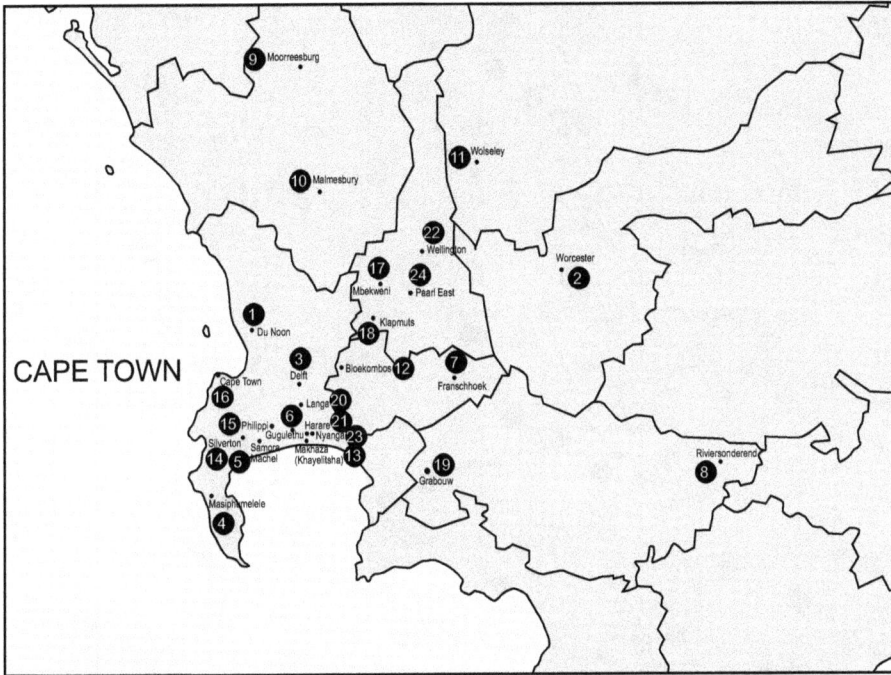

Figure 5: Collective Violence Locations, South Africa 2012–2013

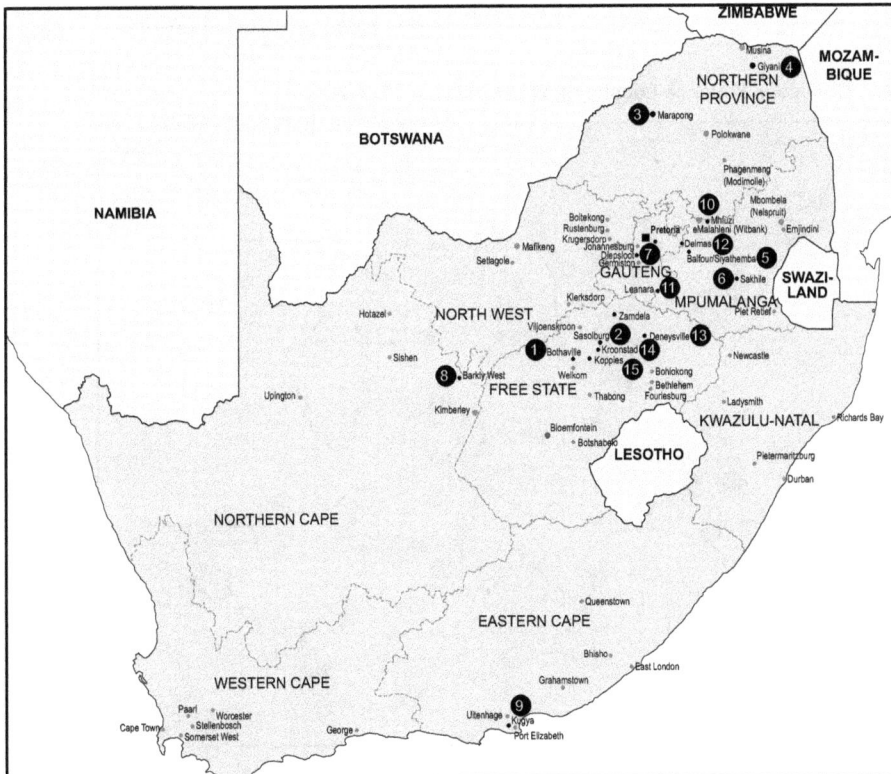

Figure 6: Collective Violence Locations, Gauteng 2012–2013

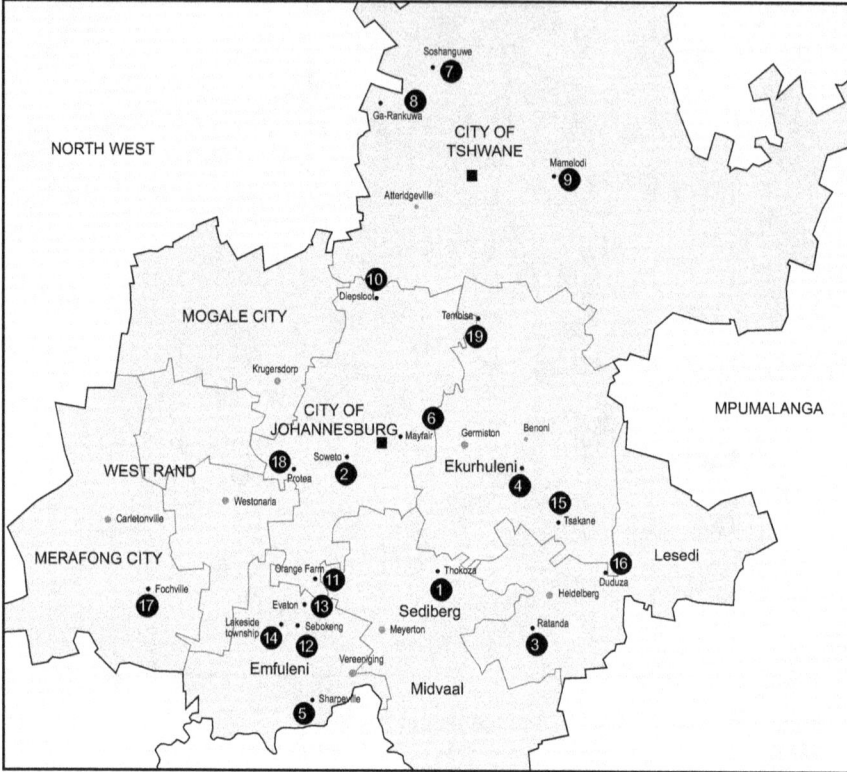

Figure 7: Collective Violence Locations, Western Cape 2012–2013

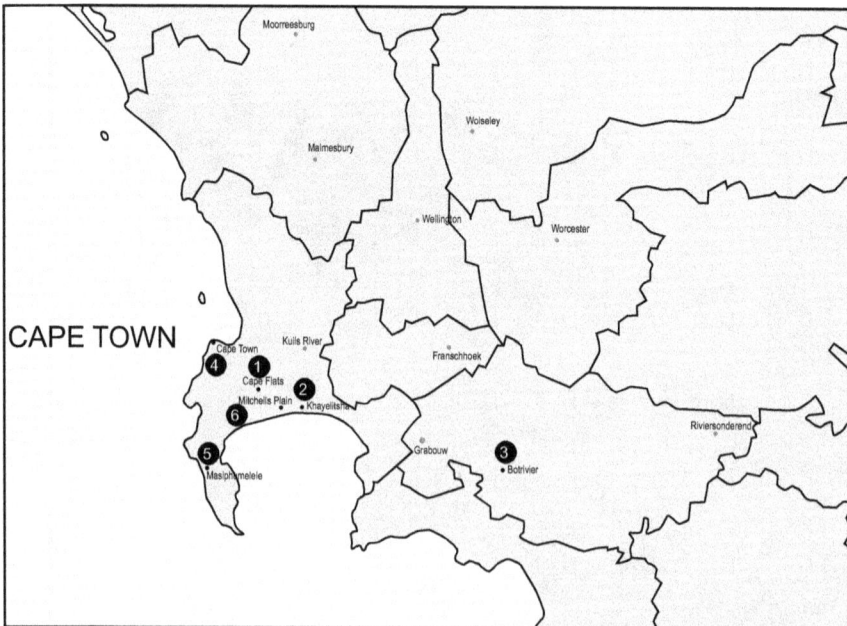

Key

Figure 1: South Africa 2005–2006
1. Viljoenskroon
2. Bothaville
3. Knysna
4. Masiphumelele
5. Cape Flats
6. Diepsloot

Figure 2: South Africa 2009–2010
1. Bothaville
2. Sasolburg
3. Marapong
4. Giyani
5. Balfour/Siyathemba
6. Sakhile
7. Diepsloot
8. Barkly West
9. Kugya
10. Mhluzi
11. Leandra
12. Delmas
13. Deneysville
14. Kroonstad
15. Koppies

Figure 3: Gauteng 2009-2010
1. Diepsloot
2. Orange Farm
3. Boipatong
4. Atteridgeville
5. Mamelodi
6. Benoni
7. Mayfair
8. Tembisa
9. Kya Sands
10. Tsakane
11. Freedom Park

Figure 4: Western Cape 2009-2010
1. Du Noon
2. Worcester
3. Delft
4. Masiphumelele
5. Samora Machel
6. Gugulethu
7. Franschhoek
8. Riviersonderend
9. Moorreesburg
10. Malmesbury
11. Wolseley
12. Bloekombos
13. Makhaza (Khayelitsha)
14. Silverton
15. Philippi

16. Cape Town
17. Mbekweni
18. Klapmuts
19. Grabouw
20. Langa
21. Harare
22. Wellington
23. Nyanga
24. Paarl East

Figure 5: South Africa 2012–2013
1. Welkom
2. Thabong
3. Odendaalsrus
4. Fouriesburg
5. Viljoenskroon
6. Botshabelo
7. Phagemeng (Modimolle)
8. Emjindini
9. Rustenburg
10. Boitekong
11. Zamdela
12. Setlagole
13. Port Elizabeth

Figure 6: Gauteng 2012-2013
1. Thokoza
2. Soweto
3. Ratanda
4. Ekurhuleni
5. Sharpeville
6. Mayfair
7. Soshanguwe
8. Ga-Rankuwa
9. Mamelodi
10. Diepsloot
11. Orange Farm
12. Sebokeng
13. Evaton
14. Lakeside township
15. Tsakane
16. Duduza
17. Fochville
18. Protea
19. Tembisa

Figure 7: Western Cape 2012-2013
1. Cape Flats
2. Khayelitsha
3. Botrivier
4. Cape Town
5. Masiphumelele
6. Mitchells Plain

19

TYPOLOGIES OF COLLECTIVE VIOLENCE

The nationwide attacks on migrants and refugees in May 2008 represent the nadir of xenophobic hostility in South Africa. There is an obvious temptation to characterize other, prior and subsequent, episodes of collective violence as "minor" incidents. Such a conclusion would be profoundly misplaced. The cumulative impact of months, indeed years, of low-level verbal and physical warfare against migrant entrepreneurs has taken a major toll on the lives and livelihoods of some of South Africa's most enterprising residents. Belligerent, discriminatory and abusive types of action have occurred. They include (a) written or verbal threats and insults directed at migrant entrepreneurs; (b) public intimidation of migrant entrepreneurs through protests or marches or other similar collective actions; (c) involuntary migrant shop closures; (d) direct physical violence against migrant store owners or their employees; (e) looting of store contents; (f) damage to the physical structure of shops, especially through arson; (g) damage or destruction of other property belonging to migrant traders, including homes and cars; (h) temporary or permanent forced displacement of migrant entrepreneurs and their families; and (i) extortion for protection by local leaders, police and residents. Looting of store goods and damage to stores were easily the most common types of action recorded.

A number of incidents are worth recalling to illustrate the nature and intensity of collective violence after 2008. Between mid-2009 and late 2010, for example, more than 20 migrants were killed and another 40 received serious injuries in various attacks.[31] Of these, at least four people were killed during a series of violent confrontations over the presence of migrant traders in the Freedom Park township of Gauteng.[32] In mid-2011, 52 shops were plundered and three burnt down in Motherwell and three shops looted and one burnt down in KwaDesi.[33] In 2012, more than 700 shops were looted and/or destroyed and over 500 migrants were displaced because of public violence in Botshabelo in the Free State province.[34] That same year, two Bangladeshi traders (described as Pakistani citizens in some accounts) suffered third-degree burns and later died after a group of assailants threw a petrol-bomb on their container store in Thokoza and blocked the store's entrance preventing their escape.[35] Three shops were then petrol-bombed during large-scale looting of Somali-owned businesses in the Valhalla Park area of Cape Town.[36]

During a particularly volatile period in Port Elizabeth in mid-2013, there was extensive vandalism, arson and plundering of an estimated 150 spaza shops operated by migrants and refugees.[37] One Somali refugee, Abdi Nasir Mahmoud Good, was publicly stoned to death while attempting to salvage his belongings from his ransacked store. Video footage was later released on YouTube showing the perpetrators, some of whom were children in school uniforms. Also in 2013, more than 200 migrant shopkeepers operating small-scale businesses in the town of Delmas, east of Johannesburg, were forced to close their stores after a spate of attacks. Four spaza shops were bombed in Mitchells Plain after their migrant owners refused to pay protection money.[38] In a bout of violence over six days in June 2014, two refugees were killed when nearly 100 migrant businesses were looted or torched in Mamelodi East outside Pretoria.[39] The violence was repeated in the Phomolong area of Pretoria two months later when three people were killed and several others wounded during a rampage that lasted for three weeks.[40] Finally, before the army was called in to contain the unrest, a Somali trader was killed and three stores were torched when migrant traders were attacked during post-election violence in Alexandra township in mid-2014.[41] As these examples of collective violence demonstrate, the scale of the attacks is sometimes sizeable and can spill over into neighbouring settlements. Looting and vandalism of migrant-owned shops have been especially common features of collective violence over the past several years. These actions, though criminal, may appear less grave when compared to severe injuries and loss of lives, but they cannot be treated as inconsequential as they impose unwarranted hardships on migrant entrepreneurs through partial or complete loss of stock and destruction of their shops and investments.

The vulnerability of migrant shopkeepers has exposed them to other invidious forms of exploitation. Some 80 migrant traders operating from Extensions 8 to 12 in Diepsloot settlement north of Johannesburg, for example, were coerced into providing payment as "protection money" to local residents to avoid damages to and pillaging of their stores during service delivery protests.[42] A Johannesburg High Court order, in response to an urgent petition on xenophobic violence in Duduza and surrounding townships of the Ekurhuleni municipality, acknowledged the culpability of a ward councillor in instigating acts of violence against Somali, Bangladeshi and Ethiopian migrant traders.[43] Migrants claimed that he stoked xenophobia and then solicited bribes in exchange for their safety.

Collective violence against migrant businesses not only shatters livelihoods of the targeted migrant groups, it impacts on South African citizens and businesses. Wholesalers, retailers and suppliers are inevitably affected when migrant business activities are disrupted or destroyed. Also, a significant proportion of migrant businesses rent business spaces from South African property owners, who lose rental income when their tenants are expelled or their premises are vandalized.[44] In addition, extensive damage to store structures degrades the existing and often meagre assets of local property owners. Other losers include poor local consumers who are forced to buy more expensive goods from larger stores or face the inconvenience of travelling longer distances to purchase necessities.

PRECIPITANTS OF VIOLENCE

It is not easy to tease out and identify intentions, motivations and underlying causes in turbulent situations, especially when relying on reportage and monitoring. Scholars researching collective violence have commonly expressed this dilemma.[45] Some things are, however, evident. Some of the violence perpetrated against migrant businesses is obviously motivated only or primarily by criminal behaviour, especially robberies and looting, but to attribute all attacks to criminal motivation (as the state seeks to do) is completely reductionist and misleading. In general, the weak structural and social position of "foreigners" in localized areas as "outsiders", combined with limited access to protection and justice, certainly makes them more vulnerable to criminal attack. In other words, the attackers may not themselves be always motivated by xenophobia but it is xenophobia that makes their targets easy prey.

While the precipitants (or triggers) for any particular incident of collective violence vary, there is a clear general pattern both in terms of the choice of targets and the selective directing of violence toward migrants and migrant businesses. Local business competitors have certainly animated some of the collective violence against migrant entrepreneurs.[46] A distinctive feature is the recent emergence and incendiary stance of loosely-formed groups, purportedly representing many or all South African small-business owners. These groups range from localized structures like the Zanokhanyo Retailers' Association operating in townships, settlements and urban areas such as Khayelitsha, to larger regional forums like the innocuously-named Greater Gauteng Business Forum. Since 2008, these groups have engaged in numerous public hate campaigns against migrant businesses, liberally using belligerent tactics ranging from forced store closures, coerced price increases, limits on the number of migrant businesses in an area, and public threats through letters or by radio. A few months after the May 2008 violence, for example, many Somali shopkeepers in Khayelitsha received threatening hand-delivered letters from the Zanokhanyo Retailers' Association ordering them to cease operating their stores.[47] In late 2010, the association again used intimidatory tactics to shut down Somali-owned shops in Khayelitsha, claiming that the terms of an agreement reached with Somali shopkeepers limiting the number of migrant businesses in the area were being violated.[48] The Middelburg Small Business Community Forum claimed credit for mobilizing local authorities after the Steve Tshwete Municipality shut down 50 Somali shops and refused to issue them with trading licences.[49] Accusing them of unfair competition and rising crime, the local forum stoked group violence against migrant-run shops in Lephalale in Limpopo in 2013 in the course of which five shops, two houses and three vehicles were razed.[50]

By early 2011, the Greater Gauteng Business Forum had become a very visible presence through its intimidation of migrant traders in the province of Gauteng. There are reports of the forum's direct involvement in campaigns to expel migrant businesses from locations such as Kathlehong, Soweto, Eldorado Park, Ramaphosa, Mamelodi and Diepsloot. The forum chairperson claimed that campaigns against "foreign traders" were "strictly business" and have "nothing to do with xenophobia or politics", but the overt reasoning to justify these group actions draws from a familiar reservoir of xenophobic beliefs and a wilful misunderstanding of the rights of migrants and refugees in South Africa.[51] Distorted ideas about migrants' presence and their impacts on South Africa are used to justify collective mobilization and violence against migrant businesses. For example, the Greater Gauteng Business Forum is reported to have stated that "these people are molesting our economy".[52] Forum members and other local business groups have expressed similar discriminatory sentiments: "We feel that foreigners who entered the country illegally or don't have a business licence to run spaza shops should leave because they are destroying our small local businesses and exploiting our people".[53] In 2013, the forum reiterated its central argument by maintaining that all migrant entrepreneurs must "go back home" because they are "here to destroy local business and people" asserting, as well, that "if nothing is done about it, there will be war".[54]

The forceful targeting of migrant businesses, particularly spaza shops, has been a common feature of anti-government service-delivery protests in various parts of the country. In 2014, for example, one-third of the violent incidents involving looting and vandalism of migrant-owned shops took place during local anti-government or anti-municipality protests. Dissatisfaction over the pace of road construction and employment of locals for infrastructure projects in Sebokeng, for example, led to efforts to forcibly oust migrant businesses.[55] Agitating for a better water supply, Hebron residents in North West province looted at least six shops in February 2014 after police cracked down on protesters. The connections between local dissatisfaction and resentment over service issues and attacks on migrant-owned shops need greater explanation. One hypothesis advanced by Abdul Hasan of the Somali Association of South Africa is that "they are targeting foreigners because we are the weaker link in the community, so they hit us to get government attention".[56]

On several occasions, other kinds of protests have spiralled into xenophobic attacks on migrant businesses.[57] More than 100 shops of Pakistani and Bangladeshi migrants were attacked over several days in early 2012 in Welkom, Odendaalsrus and Thabong, for example, when local youths went on a rampage after discussions over enhanced quotas for hiring South Africans on local mines stalled.[58] In 2013, an estimated 200 businesses were damaged and plundered in Zamdela and neighbouring Deneysville and Koppies in Sasolburg during violent agitation rejecting the amalgamation of municipalities.[59] Allegations of dumped ballot boxes, election rigging and discontent over the outcome-generated post-election unrest in Alexandra in 2014 took a swift xenophobic turn when migrant shopkeepers were viciously targeted.[60] Also in 2014, an unresolved labour dispute between the South African Municipal Workers' Union and the Metsimaholo Municipality of Free State prompted the violent public raiding of migrant businesses in Zamdela and neighbouring settlements of France and Armelia outside Sasolburg.[61]

Participants in collective violence may not always use xenophobic language while attacking migrant stores, but an underlying xenophobic rationale is often there. Migrant entrepreneurs invariably characterize the general attitudes of the local community towards them in this way. Seven shops owned by Pakistani migrants were wrecked and ransacked in Boipatong during the course of an anti-government protest in February 2010, for example. The migrants themselves described the attacks as "hateful" and some participants defended their actions by arguing that "foreigners don't support our protests, and they are living a better life than us here in our country".[62] Zamdela township's residents said that migrant businesses were targeted in early 2013 during a violent protest against the merger of Metsimaholo municipality in Sasolburg with the Ngwathe municipality near Parys because they did not "assist" the local community.[63] In Duduza, local residents justified their collective, aggressive attacks on 200 migrant-owned shops in late 2013 as follows: "They come here and steal our jobs and now they are killing our children. We cannot accept this."[64]

In other instances, there were direct triggers linked to the presence of migrants. A Somali shopkeeper was killed and all Somali traders had to evacuate Booysen Park in 2013 when local residents associated them with criminal gangs and attacked them.[65] Amandla Wethu Workers' Union members assailed many Bangladeshi, Chinese, and Pakistani-owned businesses in Mthatha in the Eastern Cape after their president claimed that South African employees were being poorly remunerated.[66] Some of the largest episodes of group violence have involved retaliatory vigilantism in response to the acts of one or two migrants. Instead of confining their response to the perpetrators, the vigilantes strike out at many or all persons of the same nationality or ethnicity as the migrant offenders, or even at all "foreigners" in the area. After a migrant shop owner in Cullinan, east of Pretoria, allegedly assaulted a child for stealing from his store, for example, local residents looted many shops owned by migrants and refugees and burnt three of their vehicles.[67] Some 400 residents of Riviersonderend struck out at all Somali-owned shops in the area after a South African resident last seen in the company of Somalis was found dead. After a migrant shopkeeper reportedly shot a local youth for stealing from his store in Jeffreys Bay in early 2008, all Somali traders were attacked and forcibly ousted from the town.[68] In 2013, in Duduza on the East Rand, after an altercation over a cellphone airtime voucher between a Somali shop owner and a local youth, who was shot, some 200 stores belonging to Somali, Ethiopian, Eritrean and Bangladeshi migrants were stripped of their contents and several structures were incinerated.[69] In Lebokwagamo near Polokwane in April 2011, residents attacked all migrants from Ethiopia living in the area, looting and damaging their homes and businesses after one of their compatriots was accused of raping a girl.[70]

While xenophobic views and actions are not espoused or approved of by all local residents of affected settlements, their prevalence suggests that they do enjoy sufficient support and that there are few deterrents. Support from local community leaders also conveys a sense of legitimation and impunity, reducing the inhibition of potential offenders and, at the same time, enhancing the "opportunistic" aspects of the violence. Even official tolerance and passivity convey ambiguous messages that are only likely to perpetuate and shore up repeated cycles of violence. In several cases, affected traders hit by such attacks have shifted to another settlement only to end up facing attacks there too. In a general sense, this rhythmic configuration of collective, public violence is only likely to preserve and reinforce the social distance between South Africans and "foreigners". Mutual distrust and suspicion between groups is an inevitable outcome of a polarized context where xenophobic sentiments and practices are commonplace. Negative attitudes about South Africans expressed by migrants and refugees are merely another expression of the high degree of detachment between groups in these communities.

OFFICIAL EVASIONS

In a stance that has now become almost customary, South African politicians and senior officials at national, provincial and municipal levels are quick to label collective violence against migrants and refugees as "opportunistic crimes", committed by "criminal elements" or "hardened criminals", while simultaneously repudiating the role of anti-foreigner prejudice.[71] At national level, individual Ministers and the Cabinet as a whole have repeatedly warned against viewing attacks on migrants and refugees as evidence of xenophobia. President Zuma recently informed South African MPs that xenophobia was not "such a huge problem in South Africa".[72] Justice Minister Jeff Radebe made a similar observation in Parliament when some 80 stores and businesses owned by migrants were looted in Diepsloot: "The criminal activities that are perpetuated by some South Africans are not a reflection of xenophobic attacks against foreigners."[73] A South African Police Services (SAPS) spokesperson insisted that "when we see children looting shops and people robbing people of their goods, it is to us a blatant sign of crime that is being excused as xenophobia".[74]

The South African government recently took the unusual step of challenging *Al Jazeera's* online coverage of the stoning to death of a Somali refugee and other violence against migrants and refugees in Port Elizabeth.[75] Government spokesperson Phumla Williams insisted that the article "painted an incorrect picture of…South Africa" and was "far from reality" and continued that "South Africa allows and welcomes foreign nationals" and has "strived to build a society based on the values of unity and togetherness".[76] With this came the standard denial of the presence of xenophobia in South Africa: "The looting, displacement and killing of foreign nationals in South Africa *should not be viewed as xenophobic attacks, but opportunistic criminal acts* [emphasis ours] that have the potential to undermine the unity and cohesiveness of our communities."[77]

Similarly, at provincial level, the Gauteng government was quick to condemn the "brutal and senseless attack" on two Bangladeshi traders in Thokoza in 2012 and urged South Africans "*to refrain from branding this attack as having been motivated by xenophobia* [emphasis ours]".[78] After more than 100 complaints of looting and vandalism of migrant shops were registered in 2013 in various parts of Gauteng, government spokesperson Williams underscored the government's concern over the "*so-called xenophobic attacks* on foreign nationals [emphasis ours]".[79] When large-scale looting and attacks on migrant-owned shops occurred in 2013 in Port Elizabeth, provincial police characterized "the motive for the attacks on foreign-owned spaza shops" as "*not xenophobic in nature, but a criminal element that has seized an opportunity* [emphasis ours]".[80] This by-now-familiar argument was wheeled out again in early 2014 when violence occurred in Mamelodi East and police personnel attributed it to "criminal elements", denying that xenophobia was a factor.

The attribution of collective violence against migrant entrepreneurs to criminals and not in any way as evidence of xenophobia rings extremely hollow when the details of many of these attacks are examined. What makes the official position especially ironic is when officials themselves articulate sentiments that reproduce the xenophobic myths that they claim do not exist. A senior official in the Department of Home Affairs, for example, is reported to have informed South African MPs that "if you go to Alexandra, you go to Sunnyside, you go everywhere, spaza shops, hair salons, everything has been taken over by foreign nationals…they displace South Africans by making them not competitive".[81] At an official meeting, then National Police Commissioner Bheki Cele characterized immigrants and refugees as "people who jump borders", were flooding into the country and destroying the livelihoods of South African informal traders: "The spazas…are better stocked than Shoprite. Our people have been economically displaced. All these spaza shops [in the townships] are not run by locals…One day our people will revolt, and we've appealed to the Department of Trade and

Industry to do something about it."[82] Former Deputy DTI Minister Elizabeth Thabethe made similarly provocative statements about the supposed negative effects of Somali entrepreneurs in late 2013 at a national conference on small, medium and micro enterprises: "You still find many spazas with African names, but when you go in to buy, you find your Mohammeds and most of them are not even registered".[83]

More recently, ANC Secretary-General Gwede Mantashe declared that the South African government was concerned about South African small businesses that were closing, having been "swallowed by foreign migrants" who "did not pay tax and comply with certain laws".[84] He informed an election campaign rally at Eldorado Park South in Johannesburg that, "if you go to Soweto, corner shops have been taken over by foreigners. We must do something about it". Responding to a wave of public criticism of his Licensing of Businesses Bill, DTI Minister Rob Davies, defended the Bill as an effort to curb illegal imports:

> All kinds of outlets [are] springing up that may well be involved in illegal imports and things of that sort…If you are found guilty of a number of offences, such as selling counterfeit goods…[and] you've been involved in illegal imports, found guilty of contravening the Foodstuffs, Cosmetics, and Disinfectants Act, been selling sub-standard products, employing illegal foreigners, or found guilty of conducting illegal business from the licensed premises, you've been doing drug trade or illegal liquor selling or anything of the sort…your licence is automatically revoked. So we say, easy in, easy out. You do any of those things, we don't want you.[85]

The Minister did not mention that existing legislation is more than able to deal with illegal imports, the employment of irregular migrants and illicit drug and liquor selling. He did not respond to criticisms that he viewed the informal economy as a hive of criminality and that the Bill was actually a frontal attack on informal business and migrant entrepreneurship.

The opinions of politicians and officials about migrant entrepreneurs often seem indistinguishable from the intolerant views of ordinary citizens and this, in turn, reinforces negative beliefs and ideas in the populace at large. Failure to curb the situation by consistently restraining offenders and imposing stringent penalties on collective violence only expands the elements of "opportunism" attached to such acts, encouraging others to participate, and reinforcing the unprotected position of migrants and refugees as "outsiders" in affected areas. Thus, photographs in the South African media in July 2012 show the Bishop Lavis (Cape Town) police "standing and doing nothing" while spaza shops were torched and looted in Valhalla Park.[86] The Western Cape Minister for Community Safety, Dan Plato, later announced in a public statement that the Independent Police Investigative Directorate would examine the case and "take necessary action where any negligence or wrongdoing is identified".[87] However, it is not clear if the case was actually investigated or disciplinary proceedings carried out against the SAPS personnel.[88]

Police passivity has been reported by migrants and the media in many episodes of violence targeting foreign-owned businesses. As far back as 2005, for example, some 150 Pakistani entrepreneurs operating spaza shops in Pietermaritzburg organized a protest march against the local police demanding accountability after a large mob looted goods worth R150,000 from one of them.[89] Refugee shopkeepers from the Democratic Republic of Congo, Ethiopia and Somalia who were forced out of Zwelethemba township near Worcester in the Western Cape in 2008 filed claims in the Equality Court in 2009 seeking redress for the unfair discrimination, xeno-phobia and inadequate protection provided by police officials during this violent episode.[90] Despite extensive looting and vandalism of Somali shops in Motherwell, Port Elizabeth, in 2013, local police said they were unable to offer protection.[91] Immigrants whose shops and homes were assailed in Wallacedene during a housing dispute in mid-2013 maintained that police personnel refused to provide assistance, insisting instead that they leave South Africa.[92] Weak, hostile or indifferent police responses provide strong incentives for repetition by reinforcing biases among existing offenders and signalling to potential offenders that migrant businesses are easy targets.

The victimization of migrant businesses through extortion for protection has also been reported. A report on policing in Khayelitsha, an area prone to regular violence against migrants and refugees, observed that local police personnel often demanded bribes from migrant traders and stole items from their stores.[93] Civil society groups accused the local police of checking immigration documents of affected traders instead of shielding them dur-ing the public violence that erupted in Mamelodi East and West in June 2014.[94] Dissatisfied with the quality and consistency of police protection, spaza owners have adopted two main strategies. First, to protect their own businesses from attack, they have entered into local agreements with the police and South African entrepreneurs that they will support their efforts to prevent any new migrant businesses opening in an area. Second, they have begun to arm themselves with weapons to defend their stores and their lives. Armed clashes between attackers and store owners have become increasingly common in recent years.

While the police are often accused of standing by in situations of collec-tive violence, they also act against migrant businesses when ordered to do so. With the tacit consent of provincial authorities, and without any prior warning, local police in Limpopo province undertook an anti-crime cam-paign called "Operation Hardstick" in 2012, ostensibly to apprehend crimi-nals and aggressively tackle illicit activities. They sealed some 600 business-es run by immigrants and refugees, confiscated their trading stock, imposed fines on them for trading without permits and, according to some accounts, detained traders as well as subjecting them to verbal xenophobic abuse.[95] Thirty displaced Ethiopians were then forced to flee when the house they were staying in was fire-bombed. The exercise was selectively enforced on migrant entrepreneurs and did not affect South African businesses in these locations. The Supreme Court, in finding against the Limpopo Government and for the Somali Association of South Africa, observed that "one is left with the uneasy feeling that the stance adopted by the authorities in relation to the licensing of spaza shops and tuck-shops was in order to induce foreign nationals who were destitute to leave our shores".[96]

Weak or lack of effective punishment for the perpetrators of violence sends permissive signals and tacit sanction. People have been arrested in various parts of South Africa over the past few years for public violence, looting, arson, malicious damage to property, possession of stolen goods and for their participation in collective violence targeting migrant businesses. But a great many have been released after verbal warnings and very few offenders have been indicted or faced harsh prison sentences. For example, in 2011, the Germiston Magistrate's Court released without any penalty 71 Kathlehong residents arrested for distributing intimidating letters threatening "drastic action" against migrant-owned businesses.[97] Again, 11 people were arrested for the death of Somali refugee Nasir Good, but none of the offenders was formally charged or faced criminal proceedings. To date, there is evidence of the prosecution and conviction of offenders in only two serious incidents. The first case involved the burglary of three migrant-owned businesses in Buhlebesizwe No. 2 village near Kwaggafontein in 2011 for which five citizens were sentenced to individual terms of 15 years by a Mpumalanga judge.[98] In the second case, one of the three accused in the murder of an Ethiopian trader, Thomas Ebamo, in 2012 was sentenced to 25 years' imprisonment in what was characterized by the presiding judge as a "savage act of xenophobia".[99] A seller of pots and carpets from his car, Ebamo had been robbed and dragged to his death after being tied to a vehicle's rear by his neck. However, these convictions and judgments are very much the exception and not the norm.

CONCLUSION

Some migrant entrepreneurs may enjoy material advantages over ordinary South Africans in settlements where they operate their informal businesses, trading stalls or spaza shops. However, their status as "foreigners" and "outsiders" in South African society makes them markedly vulnerable to constant victimization, harassment and violence. More than that, these commonplace actions magnify the sense of constant insecurity experienced by migrants and refugees, compromising the ability of victims to fully integrate into South African society. The pervasive sense of fear and insecurity

and the constant possibility of violence directed at their bodies and proper-
ties is a reality that they have to face on a daily basis in areas where they
operate their businesses. As one Somali refugee put it, "we came to this
country as refugees, because Somalia is being torn apart by war, but here
another war is taking place, one that we don't understand, but we are the
targets".[100]

The terms of the debate on the rise of migrant entrepreneurship in
South Africa have been limited and selective, reiterating (both implicitly
and explicitly) the prejudiced, xenophobic idea that non-citizens are not
entitled to police protection nor even running a small business, even if it
is enshrined in law and generated through their own initiative and inven-
tiveness.[101] Explaining collective violence through an undue emphasis on
group rivalries for limited material resources allows the culpability to be
shifted on to the attacked group, migrants and refugees in this case, thus
making the victims responsible for their own suffering. Collective violence
against migrant businesses and migrants at large becomes an inexorable,
uncontrolled feature of social reality in such a delimited stance, erasing and
minimizing options for positive change or progressive interventions leading
to the fuller acceptance of immigrants into South African society, economy
and polity.[102]

Equally importantly, when assessments of "economic competition" are
delimited on a group basis, particularly when the boundaries are drawn
around nationality, citizenship and other forms of ethnicity, then they are
rooted in discriminatory normative judgements about the different and une-
qual economic entitlements of citizens and foreigners in South Africa. The
idea of economic competition itself is defined selectively and incompletely
here, omitting the very real and stronger challenges to informal entrepreneurship posed by large grocery stores or supermarkets.[103] It is difficult to
imagine a scenario where the South African government would endorse or
impose severe limits on the expansion of large commercial/retail stores in
townships and poorer settlements on the grounds that they truncate business opportunities for small-scale South African entrepreneurs. In terms of
concrete, practical intervention, the focus turns in a reactionary manner
to curtailing migrant entrepreneurship in place of the real, urgent need to
support and enhance opportunities for *all* small entrepreneurs in marginal
settlements through new incentives and programmes.

The official idea that collective violence against migrant-owned shops
and businesses is best controlled through the imposition of tougher restrictions on migrant businesses rather than robust sanctions against perpetrators through hate-crime legislation and other measures is deeply ingrained.
So, too, is the feeling that there is no need to ease suspicions about "foreigners" and their economic activities within the country. A recent ANC
policy discussion document, for example, incongruously focused on "peace

and stability" and recommended that "by-laws need to be strengthened" in a manner that meant "non-South Africans should not be allowed to run or buy spaza shops or larger businesses".[104] The document further suggested that asylum-seekers whose refugee applications had not been finalized by the Department of Home Affairs should be ineligible to operate and manage such shops, diverging from protections granted to this vulnerable group under national and international law. ANC Western Cape Secretary Songezo Mjongile endorsed these proposals by contending that the rise of migrant entrepreneurship was the underlying cause of friction and collective violence in townships and saying it was "unnatural that nearly all shops in townships are owned by foreigners. More locals need to participate and need to be supported...it creates tension".[105]

Despite providing goods at cheaper prices to poor consumers, in affordable quantities and sometimes on credit, the success and resourcefulness of migrant entrepreneurs is regularly and often falsely attributed to the use of illegitimate practices such as the sale of expired goods and failure to pay taxes. Police Commissioner Arno Lamoer admitted to Parliament's Police Portfolio Committee that migrant and refugee entrepreneurs constituted the victims in two-thirds of crimes such as robberies committed against small businesses in the Western Cape, but held them responsible for operating shops from homes or containers without trading permits, failing to bank their earnings and sleeping in the store premises.[106] Similarly, DTI Minister Davies' defence of the Licensing of Businesses Bill argued that its basic purpose was to control illegal imports and trading when most commentators have seen it as a frontal attack on migrant entrepreneurship since, amongst other things, it requires all migrants to have business permits that cost far more than what all but a tiny minority of informal entrepreneurs can afford.

Far from reducing xenophobia in South Africa, claims that collective violence against migrant businesses are simply acts of criminality legitimize and may even incite further violence. These acts are both criminal and opportunistic, but not in the sense suggested in public and political discourses in South Africa. These acts are criminal in that they can be considered as offences under the South African penal code and undermine the rule of law. Using this logic, one may argue that those who have engaged in such acts may be considered as "criminals". South African shop owners have certainly engaged long-term, hardened offenders to get rid of their "competition" through violence, and it may even be argued that "criminals" have committed some of these acts.[107] But a strong case can be made that not all of those who have engaged in such violence have histories of criminal activity. Situations of mayhem and melee may allow some ordinary citizens to engage in such actions and the material benefits from participating in such violent actions through looting cannot be detached from the analysis. Therefore, an element of opportunism is clearly present, which is why some observers have called it "opportunistic xenophobia".[108]

Selective notions about the barriers faced by South African small-scale entrepreneurs animate this debate, as do biased ideas about migrants, their activities, and false reasons for their success. The deeply-embedded terrain of xenophobia further provides the fertile, volatile context in which a range of social, political and economic actors (including participants in violent attacks, South African traders, local councillors and, in some cases, police) have controlled the anxieties associated with the presence of migrants for their own narrow, self-serving interests. The escalating pattern of collective violence against migrants and their businesses signals the deeply-drawn divisions between insiders and outsiders, based on birth, citizenship and nationality. This highly repetitive cycle of violence targeting migrant entrepreneurs underscores the precarious status they and other immigrants hold in South African society.

Endnotes

1. United Nations High Commissioner for Refugees (UNHCR), "South Africa Takes Practical Steps to Combat Xenophobia", 2007, at http://plwww.ccr.org/46b1dc564.html.
2. R. Waldinger, H. Aldrich and R. Ward, eds., *Ethnic Entrepreneurs: Immigrant Business in Industrial Societies* (Newbury Park: Sage, 1990); J. Rath, ed., *Immigrant Businesses: The Economic, Political and Social Environment* (Basingstoke: Macmillan, 2000); J. Rath, ed., *Unravelling the Rag Trade: Immigrant Entrepreneurship in Seven World Cities* (Oxford: Berg, 2002); P. Ensign and N. Robinson, "Entrepreneurs Because They Are Immigrants or Immigrants Because They Are Entrepreneurs?" *Journal of Entrepreneurship* 20 (2011): 23-53.
3. R. Kloosterman and J. Rath, eds., *Immigrant Entrepreneurs: Venturing Abroad in the Age of Globalization* (Oxford: Berg, 2003).
4. G. Barrett, T. Jones and D. McEvoy, "United Kingdom: Severely Constrained Entrepreneurialism" In Kloosterman and Rath, *Immigrant Entrepreneurs*, pp. 101-122; M. Magatti and F. Quassoli, "Italy: Between Legal Barriers and Informal Arrangements" In Kloosterman and Rath, *Immigrant Entrepreneurs*, pp. 147-172; D. Halkias, P. Thurman, N. Harkiolakis and S. Caracatsanis, eds., *Female Immigrant Entrepreneurs: The Economic and Social Impact of a Global Phenomenon* (Farnham: Gower, 2011).
5. J. Levie and D. Smallbone, "Immigration, Ethnicity and Entrepreneurial Behavior" In *Perspectives on Entrepreneurship: Volume 1* (New York: Praeger, 2009), pp. 157-180.
6. D. Ley, "Explaining Variations in Business Performance Among Immigrant Entrepreneurs in Canada" *Journal of Ethnic and Migration Studies* 32 (2006): 743-764. C. Teixeira, L. Lo and M. Truelove, "Immigrant Entrepreneurship, Institutional Discrimination, and Implications for Public Policy: A Case Study in Toronto" *Environment and Planning C: Government and Policy* 25 (2007): 176-193.

7. S. Peberdy and C. Rogerson, "South Africa: Creating New Spaces?" In Klooster-man and Rath, *Immigrant Entrepreneurs*, pp. 79-100.
8. S. Hassim, T. Kupe and E. Worby, *Go Home or Die Here: Violence, Xenophobia and the Reinvention of Difference in South Africa* (Johannesburg: Wits University Press, 2008).
9. B. Maharaj, "Migrants and Urban Rights: Politics of Xenophobia in South African Cities" *L'Espace Politique* 8 (2009), DOI: 10.4000/espacepolitique.1402
10. J. Crush, "The Dark Side of Democracy: Migration, Xenophobia and Human Rights in South Africa" *International Migration* 38(6) (2000): 103-134; J. Crush et al., *The Perfect Storm: The Realities of Xenophobia in Contemporary South Africa*, SAMP Migration Policy Series No. 50, Cape Town, 2008; J. Crush, S. Ramachandran and W. Pendleton, *Soft Targets: Xenophobia, Public Violence and Changing Attitudes to Migrants in South Africa After May 2008*, SAMP Migration Policy Series No. 64, Cape Town, 2013.
11. J. Crush and S. Ramachandran, *Xenophobic Violence in South Africa: Denialism, Minimalism, Realism*, SAMP Migration Policy Series No. 66, Cape Town, 2014.
12. Ibid.
13. Z. Jinnah, "Making Home in a Hostile Land: Understanding Somali Identity, Integration, Livelihood and Risks in Johannesburg" *Journal of Sociology and Social Anthropology* 1 (2010): 91-99; C. Abdi, "Moving Beyond Xenophobia: Structural Violence, Conflict and Encounters with the 'Other' Africans" *Development Southern Africa* 28 (2011): 691-704; A. Ikuomola and J. Zaaiman, "We Have Come to Stay and We Shall Find All Means to Live and Work in this Country: Nigerian Migrants and Life Challenges in South Africa" *Issues in Ethnology and Anthropology* 9 (2014): 371-388.
14. A. Visser, "Race, Poverty, and State Intervention in the Informal Economy: Evidence from South Africa" PhD Thesis, New School University, New York, 2010; A. Wafer, "Informality, Infrastructure and the State in Post-Apartheid Johannesburg" PhD Thesis, Open University, 2011.
15. A. Charman and L. Piper, "Xenophobia, Criminality and Violent Entrepreneurship: Violence against Somali Shopkeepers in Delft South, Cape Town, South Africa" *South African Review of Sociology* 43 (2012): 81-105.
16. Crush et al., *Soft Targets*.
17. Ibid
18. Crush and Ramachandran, *Xenophobic Violence in South Africa*.
19. Ibid; Crush et al., *The Perfect Storm*; Crush et al., *Soft Targets*.
20. S. Martin, "Investigating Hate Crimes: Case Characteristics and Law Enforcement Responses" *Justice Quarterly* 13 (1996): 455-480; H. Wells and L. Polders, "Anti-Gay Hate Crimes in South Africa: Prevalence, Reporting Practices, and Experiences of the Police" *Agenda* 20 (2006): 20-28; P. Gerstenfeld, *Hate Crimes: Causes, Controls, and Controversies* (London: Sage Publications, 2013).
21. V. Gastrow, "Business Robbery, the Foreign Trader and the Small Shop: How Business Robberies Affect Somali Traders in the Western Cape" *South African Crime Quarterly* 43 (2013): 5-15.

22. A. Zwi, R. Garfield and A. Loretti, "Collective Violence" In E. Krug, L. Dahl-berg, J. Mercy, A. Zwi and R. Lozano, eds., *World Report on Violence and Health* (Geneva: WHO, 2002), pp. 215-229.
23. C. Tilly, *The Politics of Collective Violence* (Cambridge: Cambridge University Press, 2003).
24. J. Crush and S. Ramachandran, "Xenophobia, International Migration and Development" *Journal of Human Development and Capabilities* 11(2) (2010): 209-228; L. Landau, ed., *Exorcising the Demons Within: Xenophobia, Violence and Statecraft in Contemporary South Africa* (Johannesburg: Wits University Press, 2012).
25. R. de la Roche, "Collective Violence as Social Control" *Sociological Forum* 11 (1996): 97-128.
26. R. de la Roche, "Why Is Collective Violence Collective?" *Sociological Theory* 19 (2001): 126-144.
27. T. Monson, K. Takabvirwa, J. Anderson, T. Polzer Ngwato and I. Freemantle, "Promoting Social Cohesion and Countering Violence Against Foreigners and Other 'Outsiders'" *ACMS Report*, University of the Witwatersrand, Johannes-burg, 2012.
28. D. Everatt, *South African Civil Society and Xenophobia: Synthesis* (Strategy & Tactics and Atlantic Philanthropies: Johannesburg, 2010); Hassim, Kupe and Worby, *Go Home or Die Here*; Landau, *Exorcising the Demons Within*; South African Human Rights Commission (SAHRC), *Report on the SAHRC Investiga-tion into Issues of Rule of Law, Justice and Impunity arising out of the 2008 Violence Against Non-Nationals*, SAHRC, Johannesburg, 2010.
29. A. Harber, *Diepsloot* (Johannesburg: Jonathan Ball, 2011).
30. SAHRC, *Investigation into Issues of Rule of Law, Justice and Impunity*; J. Steinburg, "South Africa's Xenophobic Eruption", ISS Paper 169, November, 2008.
31. Consortium on Refugees and Migrants in South Africa (CoRMSA), "Protect-ing Refugees, Asylum-Seekers and Immigrants in South Africa during 2010" Johannesburg, 2011.
32. A. Mashego, "Task Team to Tackle Freedom Park Tension with Foreigners" *New Age* 25 January 2011.
33. S. Maliza, "The HRC Criticizes Attacks on Somali Shops" *Sunday Times* 27 May 2011.
34. CoRMSA, "CoRMSA Condemns Attacks on Foreign Nationals in Botshabelo", 2012 at http://www.cormsa.org.za/wp-content/uploads/2009/05/Botshobelo-xenophobic-violence.pdf.
35. S. Smillie, "Bangladeshi Traders Die After Torching" *The Star* 1 February 2012.
36. B. Margele, "Plato to Probe Bishop Lavis Police" *Cape Times* 12 July 2012.
37. South African Press Association (Sapa), "Foreigners' Shops Looted in PE" 16 September 2013; Sapa, "Somali-Owned PE Shops Re-Open after Attacks" 19 September 2013.
38. "Shops Petrol-Bombed Over 'Protection Fee'" *News24* 13 July 2013.

39. UNHCR, "UNHCR Concerned Over Recent Attacks Aimed at Foreigners Including Refugees in Mamelodi" *UNHCR News* 11 June 2014.

40. N. Makhubu, "Foreigners in Fear After Looting of Shop" *Pretoria News* 12 September 2014.

41. R. Poplak, "Hannibal Elector: From Alexandra to Zuma, via Malema: Violence, Silence & Nothing Wrong With Nkandla" *Daily Maverick* 11 May 2014.

42. CoRMSA, "Database of Violence Against Foreign Nationals in 2009-2010", 2010.

43. A. Serrao, "Hostility Against Foreigners on the Rise" *IOL News* 31 October 2013.

44. V. Gastrow and R. Amit, "Somalinomics: A Case Study on the Economics of Informal Trade in the Western Cape" ACMS Report, University of the Witwatersrand, Johannesburg, 2013.

45. J. Short and M. Wolfgang, "Perspectives on Collective Violence" In J. Short and M. Wolfgang, eds., *Collective Violence* (Transaction Publishers: New Brunswick, 2009), pp. 3-32; Tilly, *The Politics of Collective Violence*; A. Varshney, M. Tadjoeddin and R. Panggabean, "Creating Datasets in Information-Poor Environments: Patterns of Collective Violence in Indonesia, 1990-2003" *Journal of East Asian Studies* 8(3) (2008): 361-394.

46. V. Gastrow and R. Amit, "Elusive Justice: Somali Traders' Access to Formal and Informal Justice Mechanisms in the Western Cape" ACMS Report, University of the Witwatersrand, Johannesburg, 2012.

47. "Foreign Competitors Not Welcome" IRIN 17 October 2008.

48. N. Damba, "Somali shops closed down in Khayelitsha" *West Cape News* 10 October 2010.

49. J-P. Misago and M. Wilhelm-Solomon, "Evicted Somali Traders Cry Foul" *Mail & Guardian* 4 September 2011.

50. Crush and Ramachandran, *Xenophobic Violence in South Africa.*

51. "Campaign Against Foreign Township Traders Spreads" *City Press* 14 May 2011.

52. Z. Mukhuthu, "Minister's remarks rile traders" *Sowetan* 9 March 2011.

53. "Campaign Against Foreign Township Traders Spreads".

54. S. Masombuka, and A. Narsee, "Send foreigners to camps" *Times Live* 28 May 2013.

55. K. Patel, "Sebokeng's Cocktail of Joblessness, Drugs and Xenophobia" *Daily Maverick* 27 May 2013; K. Patel, "'Xenophobic' Violence Spreads, Threatens Chaos" *Daily Maverick* 31 May 2013.

56. O. Kumwenda, "South African Police Fire Buckshot at Township Rioters" *Reuters* 23 March 2010.

57. UNHCR, "UNHCR Concerned Over Recent Attacks Aimed at Foreigners."

58. "Attacks Mount on Shops Owned by Foreigners" *SABC* 5 February 2012.

59. M. Motumi, "Foreigners Run Scared in Sasolburg" *The Star* 24 January 2013; T. Nkonki, "Sasolburg Unrest Likened to Xenophobic Attacks" *Eyewitness News* 24 January 2013.

60. Poplak, "Hannibal Elector: From Alexandra to Zuma, via Malema."
61. B. Ndaba, "Mobs Loot Foreign Businesses in Zamdela" *The Star* 17 July 2014.
62. Displaced and Migrant Persons Support Programme, "Xenophobic Attacks – Boipatong, Vaal" 29 February 2010.
63. L. Sidimba, "Why Foreign Shops Were Targeted" *City Press* 27 January 2013.
64. G. Hosken, "Townships Turn on Foreign 'Killers'" *Times Live* 16 August 2013.
65. D. McDonald, "All Somali Shops in Booysen Park Looted" *News24* 30 May 2013.
66. "Foreign nationals' shops vandalized, looted in Mthatha" *SABC* 5 February 2014.
67. "Foreigners Escorted Out of Cullinan" *City Press* 19 February 2014
68. "Somali shops looted in the Eastern Cape" *Mail & Guardian* 7 October 2008.
69. K. Sosibo, "Attacks on Duduza 'Not Random'" *Mail & Guardian* 20 September 2013.
70. M. Matlala, "Ethiopian Nationals Attacked" *New Age* 20 April 2011.
71. T. Polzer and K. Takabvirwa, "Just Crime?: Violence, Xenophobia and Crime: Discourse and Practice" *SA Crime Quarterly* 33 (2010): 3-10; Crush and Ramachandran, *Xenophobic Violence in South Africa*; I. Freemantle and J-P. Misago, "The Social Construction of (Non) Crises and Its Effects: Government Discourse on Xenophobia, Immigration and Social Cohesion in South Africa" In A. Lindley, ed., *Crisis and Migration: Critical Perspectives* (New York: Routledge, 2014).
72. "Xenophobia Must Not Get Out of Hand: Zuma" *SABC* 20 June 2013.
73. K. Patel, "'Xenophobic' Violence Spreads, Threatens Chaos".
74. N. Bauer, "Diepsloot: Crime, xenophobia – or both?" *Mail & Guardian*, 28 May 2013.
75. K. Patel and A. Essa, "African Migrants Battling Rising Persecution" *Al Jazeera* 6 June 2013.
76. P. Williams, "Response to Al Jazeera: Article on South Africa" *Al Jazeera* 22 June 2013.
77. I. Hirsi, "Somali Man Stoned to Death in South Africa: Sister and Community Protest in St. Paul" *TC Daily Planet* 6 September 2013.
78. Gauteng Provincial Government, "Gauteng Condemns the Attack on Bangladeshi Nationals in Thokoza" at https://www.facebook.com/GPPremierOffice/posts/262525377152972
79. "Foreigners' Shops Looted in PE."
80. "111 Arrested for PE Protests" *Sapa* 18 September 2013.
81. C. Van der Westhuizen, "Torn Between Two Discourses" *The Star* 30 August 2011.
82. Q. Mtyala, "Cele's Xenophobic Outburst" *Cape Times* 7 October 2011.
83. "Foreign-Owned Businesses Hampering Rural Growth: DTI" *The Sowetan* 10 October 2013.
84. B. Ginindza, "ANC will Add Ministry for Small Business" *Business Report* 9 April 2014.

85. K. Radebe, "Big Brother's New Business Bill" *Moneyweb*, 20 March 2013.
86. Margele, "Plato to Probe Bishop Lavis Police."
87. Government of Western Cape, Looting of Shops: IPID Asked to Investigate Apparent Lack of Policing, 10 July 2012 at http://www.westerncape.gov.za/news/looting-shops-ipid-asked-investigate-apparent-lack-policing.
88. Margele, "Plato to Probe Bishop Lavis Police."
89. Crush et al., *The Perfect Storm.*
90. J. de Jager, "Addressing Xenophobia in the Equality Courts of South Africa" *Refuge* 28 (2011): 107-16.
91. CoRMSA, "Protecting Refugees, Asylum-Seekers and Immigrants."
92. T. Washinyira, "Cape Town: Immigrants Accuse Cops of Abuse as Their Businesses are Destroyed" *Daily Maverick* 27 June 2013.
93. Khayelitsha Commission, "Towards a Safer Khayelitsha: Report of the Commission of Inquiry into Allegations of Police Inefficiency and a Breakdown in Relations between SAPS and the Community in Khayelitsha", 2014 at http://www.khayelitshacommission.org.za/final-report.html
94. UNHCR, "UNHCR Concerned Over Recent Attacks Aimed at Foreigners."
95. M. Khoza, "Operation Hardstick: Cops Out in Force" *News24* 23 April 2012; Supreme Court, "Somali Association of South Africa and Others v Limpopo Department of Economic Development Environment and Tourism and Others (48/2014)", 2014 at http://www.saflii.org/za/cases/ZASCA/2014/143.html
96. Supreme Court, "Somali Association of South Africa and Others."
97. "Case Against 71 Kathlehong Residents Dismissed" *SABC News* 30 April 2011.
98. F. Nyaka, "Five Sentenced to Robbery of Foreign Nationals" *New Age* 19 February 2013.
99. I. Oellerman, "25 Years for 'Savage Act of Xenophobia'" *The Witness* 20 March 2013.
100. "Rioters Loot and Burn Somali-owned Shops" *The Citizen* 14 February 2007.
101. Gastrow and Amit, "Somalinomics."
102. Crush and Ramachandran, *Xenophobic Violence in South Africa.*
103. J. Crush and B. Frayne, "Supermarket Expansion and the Informal Food Economy in Southern African Cities: Implications for Urban Food Security" *Journal of Southern African Studies* 37 (2011): 781-807.
104. African National Congress (ANC), "Peace and Stability: Policy Discussion Document", 2012 at http://www.anc.org.za/docs/discus/2012/peacev.pdf
105. C. Barnes, "Cut Number of Foreign Spaza Shops – ANC" *Cape Argus* 25 June 2012.
106. "Shops Petrol-Bombed Over 'Protection Fee'."
107. Gastrow and Amit, "Somalinomics."
108. Makhubu, "Foreigners in Fear After Looting of Shop."

MIGRATION POLICY SERIES

1. *Covert Operations: Clandestine Migration, Temporary Work and Immigration Policy in South Africa (1997) ISBN 1-874864-51-9*

2. *Riding the Tiger: Lesotho Miners and Permanent Residence in South Africa (1997) ISBN 1-874864-52-7*

3. *International Migration, Immigrant Entrepreneurs and South Africa's Small Enterprise Economy (1997) ISBN 1-874864-62-4*

4. *Silenced by Nation Building: African Immigrants and Language Policy in the New South Africa (1998) ISBN 1-874864-64-0*

5. *Left Out in the Cold? Housing and Immigration in the New South Africa (1998) ISBN 1-874864-68-3*

6. *Trading Places: Cross-Border Traders and the South African Informal Sector (1998) ISBN 1-874864-71-3*

7. *Challenging Xenophobia: Myth and Realities about Cross-Border Migration in Southern Africa (1998) ISBN 1-874864-70-5*

8. *Sons of Mozambique: Mozambican Miners and Post-Apartheid South Africa (1998) ISBN 1-874864-78-0*

9. *Women on the Move: Gender and Cross-Border Migration to South Africa (1998) ISBN 1-874864-82-9.*

10. *Namibians on South Africa: Attitudes Towards Cross-Border Migration and Immigration Policy (1998) ISBN 1-874864-84-5.*

11. *Building Skills: Cross-Border Migrants and the South African Construction Industry (1999) ISBN 1-874864-84-5*

12. *Immigration & Education: International Students at South African Universities and Technikons (1999) ISBN 1-874864-89-6*

13. *The Lives and Times of African Immigrants in Post-Apartheid South Africa (1999) ISBN 1-874864-91-8*

14. *Still Waiting for the Barbarians: South African Attitudes to Immigrants and Immigration (1999) ISBN 1-874864-91-8*

15. *Undermining Labour: Migrancy and Sub-contracting in the South African Gold Mining Industry (1999) ISBN 1-874864-91-8*

16. *Borderline Farming: Foreign Migrants in South African Commercial Agriculture (2000) ISBN 1-874864-97-7*

17. *Writing Xenophobia: Immigration and the Press in Post-Apartheid South Africa (2000) ISBN 1-919798-01-3*

18. *Losing Our Minds: Skills Migration and the South African Brain Drain (2000) ISBN 1-919798-03-x*

19. *Botswana: Migration Perspectives and Prospects (2000) ISBN 1-919798-04-8*

20. *The Brain Gain: Skilled Migrants and Immigration Policy in Post-Apartheid South Africa* (2000) ISBN 1-919798-14-5

21. *Cross-Border Raiding and Community Conflict in the Lesotho-South African Border Zone* (2001) ISBN 1-919798-16-1

22. *Immigration, Xenophobia and Human Rights in South Africa* (2001) ISBN 1-919798-30-7

23. *Gender and the Brain Drain from South Africa* (2001) ISBN 1-919798-35-8

24. *Spaces of Vulnerability: Migration and HIV/AIDS in South Africa* (2002) ISBN 1-919798-38-2

25. *Zimbabweans Who Move: Perspectives on International Migration in Zimbabwe* (2002) ISBN 1-919798-40-4

26. *The Border Within: The Future of the Lesotho-South African International Boundary* (2002) ISBN 1-919798-41-2

27. *Mobile Namibia: Migration Trends and Attitudes* (2002) ISBN 1-919798-44-7

28. *Changing Attitudes to Immigration and Refugee Policy in Botswana* (2003) ISBN 1-919798-47-1

29. *The New Brain Drain from Zimbabwe* (2003) ISBN 1-919798-48-X

30. *Regionalizing Xenophobia? Citizen Attitudes to Immigration and Refugee Policy in Southern Africa* (2004) ISBN 1-919798-53-6

31. *Migration, Sexuality and HIV/AIDS in Rural South Africa* (2004) ISBN 1-919798-63-3

32. *Swaziland Moves: Perceptions and Patterns of Modern Migration* (2004) ISBN 1-919798-67-6

33. *HIV/AIDS and Children's Migration in Southern Africa* (2004) ISBN 1-919798-70-6

34. *Medical Leave: The Exodus of Health Professionals from Zimbabwe* (2005) ISBN 1-919798-74-9

35. *Degrees of Uncertainty: Students and the Brain Drain in Southern Africa* (2005) ISBN 1-919798-84-6

36. *Restless Minds: South African Students and the Brain Drain* (2005) ISBN 1-919798-82-X

37. *Understanding Press Coverage of Cross-Border Migration in Southern Africa since 2000* (2005) ISBN 1-919798-91-9

38. *Northern Gateway: Cross-Border Migration Between Namibia and Angola* (2005) ISBN 1-919798-92-7

39. *Early Departures: The Emigration Potential of Zimbabwean Students* (2005) ISBN 1-919798-99-4

40. *Migration and Domestic Workers: Worlds of Work, Health and Mobility in Johannesburg* (2005) ISBN 1-920118-02-0

41. *The Quality of Migration Services Delivery in South Africa* (2005) ISBN 1-920118-03-9
42. *States of Vulnerability: The Future Brain Drain of Talent to South Africa* (2006) ISBN 1-920118-07-1
43. *Migration and Development in Mozambique: Poverty, Inequality and Survival* (2006) ISBN 1-920118-10-1
44. *Migration, Remittances and Development in Southern Africa* (2006) ISBN 1-920118-15-2
45. *Medical Recruiting: The Case of South African Health Care Professionals* (2007) ISBN 1-920118-47-0
46. *Voices From the Margins: Migrant Women's Experiences in Southern Africa* (2007) ISBN 1-920118-50-0
47. *The Haemorrhage of Health Professionals From South Africa: Medical Opinions* (2007) ISBN 978-1-920118-63-1
48. *The Quality of Immigration and Citizenship Services in Namibia (2008) ISBN 978-1-920118-67-9*
49. *Gender, Migration and Remittances in Southern Africa* (2008) ISBN 978-1-920118-70-9
50. *The Perfect Storm: The Realities of Xenophobia in Contemporary South Africa* (2008) ISBN 978-1-920118-71-6
51. *Migrant Remittances and Household Survival in Zimbabwe* (2009) ISBN 978-1-920118-92-1
52. *Migration, Remittances and 'Development' in Lesotho* (2010) ISBN 978-1-920409-26-5
53. *Migration-Induced HIV and AIDS in Rural Mozambique and Swaziland* (2011) ISBN 978-1-920409-49-4
54. *Medical Xenophobia: Zimbabwean Access to Health Services in South Africa* (2011) ISBN 978-1-920409-63-0
55. *The Engagement of the Zimbabwean Medical Diaspora* (2011) ISBN 978-1-920409-64-7
56. *Right to the Classroom: Educational Barriers for Zimbabweans in South Africa* (2011) ISBN 978-1-920409-68-5
57. *Patients Without Borders: Medical Tourism and Medical Migration in Southern Africa* (2012) ISBN 978-1-920409-74-6
58. *The Disengagement of the South African Medical Diaspora* (2012) ISBN 978-1-920596-00-2
59. *The Third Wave: Mixed Migration from Zimbabwe to South Africa* (2012) ISBN 978-1-920596-01-9
60. *Linking Migration, Food Security and Development* (2012) ISBN 978-1-920596-02-6

61. *Unfriendly Neighbours: Contemporary Migration from Zimbabwe to Botswana* (2012) ISBN 978-1-920596-16-3

62. *Heading North: The Zimbabwean Diaspora in Canada* (2012) ISBN 978-1-920596-03-3

63. *Dystopia and Disengagement: Diaspora Attitudes Towards South Africa* (2012) ISBN 978-1-920596-04-0

64. *Soft Targets: Xenophobia, Public Violence and Changing Attitudes to Migrants in South Africa after May 2008* (2013) ISBN 978-1-920596-05-7

65. *Brain Drain and Regain: Migration Behaviour of South African Medical Professionals* (2014) ISBN 978-1-920596-07-1

66. *Xenophobic Violence in South Africa: Denialism, Minimalism, Realism* (2014) ISBN 978-1-920596-08-8